every teenager's
little black book
on how to win a
friend to christ

by blaine bartel

every teenager's
little black book
on how to win a
friend to christ

by blaine bartel

Harrison House
Tulsa, Oklahoma

Unless otherwise indicated, all Scripture quotations are taken from the *New King James Version* of the Bible.

Scripture quotations marked (NIV) are taken from *The Holy Bible: New International Version®* NIV®. Copyright © 1973, 1978, 1984 by International Bible Society. Used by permission of Zondervan Publishing House. All rights reserved.

14 13 12   15 14 13 12 11 10 9

Every Teenager's Little Black Book on How To Win a Friend to Christ
ISBN 13: 978-1-57794-628-1
ISBN 10: 1-57794-628-6
Copyright © 2004 by Blaine Bartel
P.O. Box 691923
Tulsa, Oklahoma 74179

Published by Harrison House, Inc.
P.O. Box 35035
Tulsa, Oklahoma 74153

Printed in the United States of America. All rights reserved under International Copyright Law. Contents and/or cover may not be reproduced in whole or in part in any form without the express written consent of the Publisher.

contents

Live

- 4 Do's That Affect Sinners   1
- 3 Attitudes That Make You a Hypocrite   3
- 3 Things That Will Turn Off Your Family   5
- 5 Scriptures for Living Right   7
- 4 Fears You Must Conquer Every Day   9

Love

- 3 Things God's Love Does to People   12
- 5 Signs a Relationship Is Centered on the Love of God   14
- 3 Practical Ways To Show God's Love to a Sinner   16
- 3 Things Love is Not   18
- 7 Things God Did in Loving Us   20

contents (continued)

Learn

- 3 Stereotypes People Have About Christians — 23
- 5 Ways To Attract New Friends — 25
- 3 Steps To Lead a Person to Christ — 27
- 5 Things You Should Know About Sinners — 29
- 5 Scriptures That Promise Salvation — 31

Lift

- 3 Messages That Lift People Up — 35
- 4 Promises To Lift You Up — 37
- 4 Differences Between Confidence and Arrogance — 39
- 3 Ways To Lift Jesus Up in Your World — 41
- 3 Ways To Lift Up a Person Through Prayer — 43

contents (continued)

Listen

- 4 Reasons It's Critical That You Listen to People — 46
- 7 Ways To Help a Suicidal Person — 48
- 3 Important Steps To Take if You've Sinned Sexually — 50
- 3 Things To Say to a Victim of Divorce — 52
- 5 Things an Addict Needs To Know — 54

Lead

- 3 Qualities To Choose in Order To Be a Leader — 57
- 3 Reasons Leadership Creates Evangelism — 59
- 3 Things That Will Make You a Humble Leader — 61
- 3 Reasons It's Cool To Make Good Money — 63
- 4 Most Important Destinations of Every Leader — 65

4 DO'S THAT AFFECT SINNERS

The Bible encourages us in James 1:22 to be "doers of the word, and not hearers only." What you say is important, but what you do will give you the right to say it. Here are 4 do's that you must do to influence those around you who do not know Jesus.

1. **Do be generous.** The Bible says in Proverbs 19:4 that a generous man has many friends. Seek to help meet physical needs of people, and they will eventually trust you with their spiritual needs as well.

2. **Do live purely.** If you have an immoral lifestyle, your words will fall on deaf ears. Your commitment to have pure relationships with people proves your testimony of a pure relationship with God.

3. **Do be real.** Have fun. Tell jokes. Enjoy life. Listen to music. Go to good movies. Play practical jokes. You get my drift. Don't try to be so religious that you fail to relate to people. Remember, Jesus was criticized for hanging around sinners, yet kept Himself separate in His actions.

4. **Do be patient.** Think about all that God and people put up with in getting your life on track. You do not have the right to give up on anybody!

3 ATTITUDES THAT MAKE YOU A HYPOCRITE

Jesus constantly warned people against living a hypocritical life. He knew that hypocrites would cause the greatest damage to the kingdom of God. The word *hypocrite* in the Greek language means to be an actor. Christianity is not a "part" you play on Sunday morning, reverting back to the real you the rest of the week. Beware of these 3 attitudes that every hypocrite has.

1. **Being careless.** "Who cares what people think about what I do in my personal life? It's none of their business." If you don't care about how your actions affect others, you are on your way to hypocrisy.

2. **Being unteachable.** "Don't try to tell me what to do or how to live. I will make up my own mind independent of others." This kind of thinking puts you on a dangerous

road to ruin. God puts people around us to help guide and protect us. Don't despise their counsel.

3. **Comparing.** "Well, I'm not as bad as a lot of people I see in the church." This attitude was prevalent in the Pharisees in Jesus' time. These religious hypocrites were always comparing themselves to others who they felt were less spiritual. Their appearances to people were more important than how they appeared to God.

3 THINGS THAT WILL TURN OFF YOUR FAMILY

My wife, Cathy, and I have had the joy of leading many of our family members to Christ over the years. Along the way, we have also made a few mistakes that we had to overcome. Here are 3 things that you must avoid to effectively reach your family members with the gospel.

1. **Constant preaching.** Even Jesus would preach for a while and then leave and let people have time to process what He said. Choose your opportunities to share the message of Christ carefully.

2. **Separation.** Don't separate from participating in family activities like dinners, vacations, and other outings. The more you develop good relationships with them, the greater the opportunity you will have to speak into their lives.

3. **Pride.** Be quick to admit that you are not perfect and will still make mistakes from time to time. Sinners don't expect Christians to live lives of perfection, but they do expect honesty and humility.

5 SCRIPTURES FOR LIVING RIGHT

David said in Psalm 119:11, "Your word I have hidden in my heart, that I might not sin against You." If we are going to live consistently righteous lives, it is important to have the standard of God's Word before us. It is knowing and reminding ourselves of His Word that will give us the strength and grace to live out our Christian life to its fullest. Here are 5 Scriptures to keep before your eyes and in your heart at all times.

1. "Having your conduct honorable among the Gentiles, that when they speak against you as evildoers, they may, by your good works which they observe, glorify God in the day of visitation" (1 Peter 2:12).

2. "If anyone among you thinks he is religious, and does not bridle his tongue but deceives his own heart, this one's religion is useless" (James 1:26).

3. "No temptation has overtaken you except such as is common to man; but God is faithful, who will not allow you to be tempted beyond what you are able, but with the temptation will also make the way of escape, that you may be able to bear it" (1 Cor. 10:13).

4. "Though I speak with the tongues of men and of angels, but have not love, I have become sounding brass or a clanging cymbal" (1 Cor. 13:1).

5. "And one of you says to them, 'Depart in peace, be warmed and filled,' but you do not give them the things which are needed for the body, what does it profit?" (James 2:16).

4 FEARS YOU MUST CONQUER EVERY DAY

Fear is the primary tactic of your enemy, the devil. All through the Bible, we are told to "fear not." Fear will immobilize you and stop you from reaching your goals and full potential. You conquer your fears by studying, speaking, and acting on the Bible, God's Word. When you do, you will conquer these 4 kinds of fear every day.

1. **Fear of failure.** This lie tells you God is not strong enough to help you succeed, and it is perhaps the greatest attack of fear.

2. **Fear of the future.** This lie compels you to believe God is unable to see what lies ahead for you and to direct you in every step.

3. **Fear of the past.** This haunting deception says that because of where you or your family has come from, God is unable to make everything good today. (2. Cor. 5:17.)

4. **Fear of comparison.** This lie tries to talk you into believing God favors someone else more because that person appears to be doing better than you. The enemy wants you to believe God has given up on you.

3 THINGS GOD'S LOVE DOES TO PEOPLE

We cannot really love others the way God intended unless we have embraced His love for us. You cannot give something away that you do not have in the first place. God wants you to be filled to overflowing with His love so that you can pour out His goodness to others. Here are 3 things God's love will do for you and for those you have the opportunity to influence.

1. **God's love covers all sin.** Proverbs says that love covers a multitude of sin. There is no sin too great that, if you sincerely repent and are sorry, God will not remove as if it never existed. People need to know that the blood Jesus shed on the cross has the power to cleanse even the worst of sinners.

2. **God's love covers all people**. Republicans. Democrats. Independents. Americans. Canadians.

Chinese. Rich. Poor. Famous. Obscure. Red. Yellow. Black. White. As the song goes, we are all precious in His sight. In God's eyes, we are all one class of people. His creation. He loves us all without discrimination.

3. **God's love covers all the time.** Going to church is awesome. I believe it ought to be a weekly habit in our lives. But God's love is available to us and to others 7 days a week. Don't wait for Sunday for God to minister to you. Don't wait for Sunday to reach out to someone around you. His love is always in the now!

5 SIGNS A RELATIONSHIP IS CENTERED ON THE LOVE OF GOD

When you first meet someone you are attracted to, there is usually a warm fuzzy feeling inside. Your heart pounds and maybe you even get goose bumps, but these feelings shouldn't be confused for God's love. You may have a "crush" or "puppy love." However, God's love is much deeper and more sincere. Here are 5 signs to tell if you are in God's love.

1. You love the other person for who he or she is rather than what you get from the person. God freely gave us His Son with no strings attached. (John 3:16.)

2. You have Christ at the center of your relationship. (Matt. 6:33.) When Jesus is at the center of all you do, your conduct will never bring you shame or regret.

3. You are waiting until marriage for any physical relationship. Love is patient and willing to do what is right before God and best for the relationship. (1 Cor. 13:4.)

4. You respect the other person's feelings and wishes. Love never pushes someone to compromise what he or she believes is right. (1 Cor. 13:5.)

5. Love seeks to serve the other person rather than be served. (Phil. 2:3,4.)

Use these 5 benchmarks to measure your relationship to see whether it is built on God's love or human lust.

3 PRACTICAL WAYS TO SHOW GOD'S LOVE TO A SINNER

Most people who have lost their way in America have heard many a preacher, either in church, on television or radio, or even on the streets of their city. They know they have sinned and come short of God's standard. It's going to take more than just more preaching. Jesus preached, but He also showed His love in practical ways. Here are some examples He set for us.

1. **Jesus fed the multitude.** Why? Because people need food to live and because most people happen to like food! Why not ask a friend who doesn't know Christ out for dinner at a nice restaurant? It's neutral turf. A free meal. It's all good!

2. **Jesus healed the sick.** The Bible says those who believe will lay hands on the sick and they shall

recover. (Mark 16:18.) The next time a friend, family member, or coworker complains about some kind of pain or discomfort, offer to pray for them right there. You are not the healer, but you are inviting the Healer to bring His power into their lives.

3. **Jesus washed His disciples feet.** He came to serve, not to be served. What could you do for someone you hope to influence for Christ? Help them in their yard? Clean their car? Assist them with homework? Servanthood is one of the keys that opens the door of the gospel in the lives of people.

3 THINGS LOVE IS NOT

Many times, people misunderstand what true love is all about. It is quite common for people to assume that love is some icky-sweet emotion we feel and has nothing to do with intellect or common sense. Psalm 85:10 says that mercy and truth meet together. Truth, honesty, and standards must always be applied in showing God's love to others. God loves us, but He also requires us to respond to Him appropriately. Here are 3 things that love is not.

1. **Love is not a doormat.** Love is never a license for people in your life to use or abuse you in any way. Jesus always stood up to abusive people like the Pharisees.

2. **Love is not sexual.** In fact, if you really love someone, you will not have sex before marriage. Sex in marriage is simply a physical expression of love

that already exists in the hearts of two people who have committed their lives to one another forever.

3. **Love is not an emotion.** Just because you don't "feel" God's love one day, doesn't mean He has stopped loving you. I don't physically live with my parents anymore. But just because I don't feel their love each day, doesn't mean they have stopped loving me. The Bible promises that God's love will never fail you. (1 Cor. 13:8.)

7 THINGS GOD DID IN LOVING US

God did not love us in word only. There wasn't a thundering voice from heaven one day for all of humanity to hear: "I am God. I love you. Any questions?" No, He has proved His love to us in so many ways. Here are 7 ways we should never forget.

1. He sent His only Son to pay the penalty of sin for us all. (John 3:16.)

2. He promised us the power of the Holy Spirit to live this life for Him every day. (Acts 1:8.)

3. He gave us the Church so that we would not have to make it through life by ourselves. (1 Cor. 12:27.)

4. He gave us His Word to guide us, strengthen us, and inspire us each day. (Ps. 119:105.)

5. He gave us gifts and talents that will bless others and prosper us. (Prov. 18:16.)

6. He promised to never allow us to be tempted or tested beyond our abilities to resist and overcome. (1 Cor. 10:13.)

7. He gave us the gift of heaven. Even on our worst days on this earth, we have the promise of eternal life and an eternal city with no pain, no tears…only good! (Rev. 21:4.)

[LEARN]

3 STEREOTYPES PEOPLE HAVE ABOUT CHRISTIANS

Like it or not, as a Christian you have to be prepared to overcome misperceptions that people in the world have about Christianity. Some of you may remember a popular sketch on "Saturday Night Live" that featured "The Church Lady," played by Dana Carvey. This judgmental character represented everything the world hates about religion and the church. Here are 3 common stereotypes we can overcome by living out our faith in a real and genuine way.

1. **"Christians think they're all perfect."** We can overcome this stereotype by being quick to acknowledge God's grace and forgiveness in our lives. Paul reminded the church that, of all sinners, he was chief! We must humbly acknowledge that without God's incredible mercy, we would all be lost.

2. **"Christians think they know everything."** We conquer this stereotype by simple being honest when we don't have an answer for someone. If you're talking about God with a friend and they bring up something you're not sure about, just admit you don't know the answer but will do some research and try to find out. Your not knowing everything about God doesn't make Him any less real!

3. **"Christians don't have any fun."** This one is easy. Have fun and enjoy your life. Fun isn't getting drunk or high, or getting into bed with a new person every weekend. Fun is having great friends who don't need artificial activities to enjoy life!

5 WAYS TO ATTRACT NEW FRIENDS

Lee Iacocca says, "Success comes not from what you know, but from who you know and how you present yourself to each of those people."[1] Good friendships are vital to success. Maybe you are in need of some good friends.

Here are 5 ways to attract new friends.

1. **Smile.** Turn that frown upside down. This gesture may be small, but it packs a powerful punch. Showing those pearly whites is a magnet to new friends (be sure those pearls are white). (Prov. 18:24.)

2. **Listen.** Let others talk about themselves, then respond. When someone else is talking, don't be thinking about what you're going to say. Give the person your ear and thoughts. (Prov. 17:28.)

3. **Be dependable.** Be there for others during the good and the bad. Anyone can be there for the fun times, but only a friend will be there when things get rough.

4. **Keep your word.** If you say you are going to do something, do it. Keep your word even if you don't feel like it. If you can't keep a promise, then don't make it. It's better to under-promise and overachieve. (Prov. 11:3.)

5. **Help others succeed.** Be others-minded. Ask yourself, "How can I help this person?" Then do something about it. If you have this mindset, you will attract so many friends you won't know what to do.

3 STEPS TO LEAD A PERSON TO CHRIST

Winning people to Christ is one of the easiest things to do if you just know how. I've had the chance to do it hundreds of times. All it really takes is a gentle boldness, and once you do it once, it only gets easier. Here are 3 steps to remember.

1. **Cut to the chase and ask.** At some point during your conversation with someone about God, stop everything and look them square in the eye and ask, "How would you like to be sure your sins are forgiven and know Jesus as your Lord and Savior?" More times than not, their answer will be, "Sure, I'd like to know that."

2. **Stop everything and pray.** Don't wait another second. Tell them that they can pray right now and make their heart right with God. You lead the prayer

and have them repeat: "Father in heaven, thank You for sending Jesus to die for my sins. I confess Jesus as my Lord and Savior. I believe He is alive and is coming to live in me now. Thank You for forgiving all my sins and giving me a brand-new heart, a heart that wants to please You. In Jesus' name. Amen."

3. **Do your follow through.** Get them to church. Show them in Scripture the importance of water baptism. Teach them how to read their Bible and pray. They're baby Christians, and you'll have to help them learn to walk.

5 THINGS YOU SHOULD KNOW ABOUT SINNERS

Jesus said in Matthew 4:19, "Follow Me and I'll make you fishers of men." Good fishermen study all they can about how to successfully catch fish. They know what kind of bait to use, the right time of day, where in the lake to go, and the proper techniques needed to reel in the big one when it bites into the hook. We must be just as diligent and wise in our attempts to reach people. Here are 5 things you need to know about sinners.

1. No matter how happy and confident they appear on the outside, deep inside they are empty and searching.

2. When they appear the most stubborn and hard towards your message, they are likely very close to breaking. Don't give up.

3. Their eyes can be opened to truth and the reality of God through your prayers.

4. Most of them already believe in God. They need someone to show them the next step.

5. They are caught better alone than in groups. Try to get with them one on one.

5 SCRIPTURES THAT PROMISE SALVATION

It is the Word of God that will speak the strongest to people who need Christ. The Bible says that God watches over His Word to perform it. (Jer. 1:12.) Here are 5 key Scriptures that will arm you with the knowledge you need to present the gospel effectively to any person.

1. "For all have sinned and fall short of the glory of God" (Rom. 3:23). People must see that our sin separates us from God.

2. "For the wages of sin is death, but the gift of God is eternal life in Christ Jesus our Lord" (Rom. 6:23). People must see that Jesus is the bridge back into relationship with God.

3. "That if you confess with your mouth the Lord Jesus, and believe in your heart that God has raised Him from the dead, you will be saved" (Rom. 10:9). People must see that they must confess Jesus as Lord and Master of their life, believing He rose from the dead, to be saved.

4. "Not forsaking the assembling of ourselves together, as is the manner of some, but exhorting one another, and so much the more, as you see the Day approaching" (Heb. 10:25). People must see the importance of being a part of the Body of Christ by plugging into a local church with other believers.

5. "But he who received the seed on stony places, this is he who hears the word and immediately receives it with joy; yet he has no root in himself, but endures only for a while. For when tribulation or persecution

arises because of the word, immediately he stumbles" (Matt. 13:20,21). People must understand that Satan will try to steal the seed of God's Word that has been planted in their heart. It's up to them to put their roots down deep and resist Satan's lies.

3 MESSAGES THAT LIFT PEOPLE UP

We grow up in a down world. Comedian Jerry Seinfeld pokes fun of parents who are always using the word *down* with their children. "Get down!" "Settle down." Quiet down." "Turn that thing down!" You get the point. Many of the messages people hear in our world are not very positive. The nightly news is full of stories of war, crime, and tragedy. When you have a message of something that encourages, you are sure to stand out from the crowd. Here are 3 messages you can share that will lift a person up.

1. **"God created you to succeed in life."** But like any created thing, you must find out exactly what you were created to do. A hammer isn't very good at being a screwdriver. But it's powerful when used for its creative purpose.

2. **"No matter what you've done, Jesus Christ loves you without conditions."** The Bible says that while we were yet sinners, Christ died for us. (Rom. 5:8.) When we were at our worst, Jesus gave us His very best.

3. **"Heaven is a little like earth, without the bad days."** The Bible talks about streets, trees, and rivers in heaven. So there are similarities to earth. Yet it promises no pain and no tears! It is absent of tragedy, depression, and temptation. And God has a mansion prepared for every one of His children. (John 14:2; Rev. 21:4, 21; Rev. 22:1, 2.)

4 PROMISES TO LIFT YOU UP

If you are going to be a lifting agent in the lives of others, you must first be lifted up yourself. As powerful as a forklift is, it will not lift anything if its gasoline tank is empty. Similarly, you are built by God to do heavy lifting, but you can't let your spiritual fuel run dry. Here are 4 promises that I speak out loud in my prayer times and then look to walk out each day in my life. Make each one your promise too.

1. "What then shall we say to these things? If God is for us, who can be against us?" (Rom. 8:31). If God is always on your side, you are always a majority.

2. "You are of God, little children, and have overcome them, because He who is in you is greater than he who is in the world" (1 John 4:4). If the Greater One is in you, everything else you will face in life is less.

3. "Now to Him who is able to do exceedingly abundantly above all that we ask or think, according to the power that works in us" (Eph. 3:20). God is at work in my life, doing things beyond my wildest imaginations.

4. "And my God shall supply all your need according to His riches in glory by Christ Jesus" (Phil. 4:19). There is nothing I need that God has not already supplied or is currently in process of supplying.

4 DIFFERENCES BETWEEN CONFIDENCE AND ARROGANCE

Some people think that confidence is pride. You can be confident and very humble. Pride is confidence in the wrong things. True confidence comes from a solid foundation of knowing who you are in Christ. Look at these 4 differences between confidence and arrogance, and check up on yourself.

1. Confidence is security in who we are in Christ. Arrogance is self-reliance because of what we have, who we know, or what we have done.

2. Confidence is knowing that "we can do all things through Christ Jesus" versus trusting what we can do ourselves. (Phil. 4:13.)

3. Confidence is knowing our past is forgiven by God and we are in good standing with Him by faith. Arrogance is confidence in our works and our righteousness. (Eph. 2:8.)

4. Confidence is knowing that God is on our side, and therefore, it doesn't matter who is against us. Arrogance is security from circumstances and our own resources. (Rom. 8:31.)

3 WAYS TO LIFT JESUS UP IN YOUR WORLD

How do I lift Jesus up in my world? Wear a big Christian T-shirt that says, "You're going to hell—ask me how!" Right? Well, maybe not. Not to say that the entire Christian T-shirt industry needs to shut down, but maybe just some of it. The world is looking for more of a witness than a cute little message printed on 100% cotton. There are real ways that you can lift up Jesus in a real world. Here are a few.

1. **Go the extra mile in all your work.** Whether it's a job at McDonald's, early morning cheerleading or football practice, a biology class, or chores for your parents, give all you have and a little extra in all you do. This practice, when done consistently, will eventually provoke questions by curious observers, giving you the chance to share your reasons and faith.

2. **Put a watch on your words.** Guard your tongue, seeking to edify, encourage, and promote wholesome conversation. Refuse to gossip and betray the trust people have in your friendship. You will stand out from the crowd and will soon be given the chance to explain why.

3. **Break out of your comfort zone.** Help a stranger in need. Introduce yourself to a neighbor. Take a coworker out for lunch. Make a new friend. Each time you step into the life of someone else, incredible opportunities to share Christ are likely to follow.

3 WAYS TO LIFT UP A PERSON THROUGH PRAYER

Random prayers, unfounded in Scripture, are a risk at best. Why waste your time praying for something you're not really sure God is going to answer? I believe you can pray confident prayers based on a knowledge of God's will through His Word and get answers. Here are some examples.

1. "The harvest truly is plentiful, but the laborers are few" (Matt. 9:37). Pray and ask God to send Christian laborers into the lives of people you are praying will come to the knowledge of the truth.

2. "And I will give you the keys of the kingdom of heaven, and whatever you bind on earth will be bound in heaven, and whatever you loose on earth will be loosed in heaven" (Matt. 16:19). You have authority

from Jesus to bind up the specific things you see that are trying to deceive and destroy the person you're praying for. You can also loose God's power, love, and even His angels to effect their lives for Christ.

3. "As it is written, I have made you a father of many nations, in the presence of Him whom he believed—God, who gives life to the dead, and calls those things which do not exist as though they did" (Rom. 4:17). The Bible tells us that we have the faith of God and our spiritual father Abraham. Therefore, we can "call those things that be not as though they were." Call the person you are praying for "saved, serving God, and sold out to kingdom purposes" through the eyes of faith.

4 REASONS IT'S CRITICAL THAT YOU LISTEN TO PEOPLE

Many times, the best preaching and teaching that Christ did was a direct result of listening to someone. People would come to Him with sometimes simple and other times very difficult questions. The Holy Spirit would give Jesus the answer every time. James 1:19 tells us to "be quick to listen, slow to speak." A listening heart attracts many friends and will always be rewarded with wisdom from heaven. Here are 4 reasons to have a listening heart.

1. Listening gives you time to fully evaluate a person's situation before you pass on counsel or advice that is premature.

2. Listening tells the person you care. It says that person is important and you are not in a rush to get them down the road.

3. Listening gives you time to hear from God. The Lord will speak to you clearly when you take unselfish interest in the lives of others.

4. God believes in listening. What do you think He's doing when we pray? That's why He gave us 2 ears and 1 mouth. We ought to listen twice as much as we talk.

7 WAYS TO HELP A SUICIDAL PERSON

Believe it or not, there are people you know and meet every day that battle severe discouragement and depression. Some even feel like the life they have isn't worth living. Given the opportunity, God can use each of us to help a discouraged soul find purpose and meaning that will create a future worth living for. Here are some ways you can help a person who seems to have lost the will to go on.

1. Never treat talk or hints of suicide lightly. Whether they are actually serious or not, any discussion of ending life deserves serious and immediate attention.

2. Do not leave this person alone. You stay with them until they are back in the care of their family or guardian.

3. Encourage them from the Word of God. Jeremiah 29:11 promises them a future if they will put their trust in Christ.

4. Pray with them for God to intervene, and allow Him to give you the words to say at the end of your prayer.

5. Help them find pastoral counsel and/or a professional Christian counselor to help them learn to overcome depression.

6. Be sure that they have no access to any weapons or opportunities to hurt themselves.

7. Provide regular follow up in your friendship, supplying them with tapes, books, and other encouraging material.

3 IMPORTANT STEPS TO TAKE IF YOU'VE SINNED SEXUALLY

If you have sinned sexually, it's important to realize that God isn't mad at you. Read the story in John 8:1-11 about how Jesus responded to the woman caught in adultery. He didn't condemn her. He forgave her and told her to go and sin no more. Don't be afraid to go to God like Adam and Eve, who hid from Him in the Garden. (Gen. 3:8.)

Here are 3 steps to help you get back on your feet if you have sinned sexually.

1. **Repent.** (1 John 1:9.) This means to do a 180-degree turn from the direction you were going. Notice, this verse says He will forgive and cleanse you.

2. **Reject condemnation from the devil.** The Holy Spirit never condemns; He only convicts. Condemnation is a feeling of hopelessness. Conviction is a stirring to repent and move forward in God. (Rom. 8:1-4.)

3. **Restore yourself spiritually by seeking godly counsel.** Find a spiritual leader in your life, such as a parent, youth pastor, or youth leader you can confide in and receive godly counsel and encouragement from. (James 5:16; Prov. 28:13.)

Put these steps into practice, and you will be on course to recovery and to even greater spiritual heights than before.

3 THINGS TO SAY TO A VICTIM OF DIVORCE

According to national statistics, nearly half of all marriages in America have their last words in a court of law. The divorce court—a place where two people give up. Oftentimes, those that are hurt the most had nothing to do with the marriage in the first place. Children of divorced parents are forced to deal with a lot of very adult issues at a young age. Here are 3 things you can say to help.

1. **"Anytime you need to vent, I'm here."** Often a person just needs to talk things out and needs someone like you to listen. Sure, God will use you to provide wisdom and encouragement, but an attentive ear may be the most important gift you can give.

2. **"Unforgiveness is a choice to hurt yourself even more."** As much as you don't feel like it, you

must make the decision to forgive your parents. Not forgiving them only builds up the poison of bitterness and resentment that will infect all of your other relationships. For your own sake, forgive and begin to move on to all that God has for you.

3. **"None of this is your fault."** Parents have the power to make the right choices in life and have no one to blame but themselves for their decisions. Although feelings of guilt will try to attach themselves to you, resist each and every one—they don't belong to you!

5 THINGS AN ADDICT NEEDS TO KNOW

Whether it's street drugs, script pills, alcohol, or sniffing glue, what may begin as a really great high can, over a short period of time, become a terribly destructive addiction. Addiction sneaks up on its victims like a ghost in the night. The costs are enormous: family, friends, career, money, and finally, life. So where do you start in trying to help someone who's hooked? Here is a good place to start.

1. God promises them a way out if they'll commit to do their part. (2 Cor. 10:4.)

2. They can't possibly do it alone. It may be a 12-step program or a church recovery group, but they will need the support of friends and professional help.

3. Cravings, in most cases, won't leave overnight, but will draw down when battled consistently over time until victory is complete. They didn't become an addict overnight, and freedom will demand a fight.

4. They must replace old thought patterns that got them into trouble with Scripture from the Word of God that has been memorized and quoted daily. Even Jesus resisted Satan by speaking the Word of God. (Matt. 4:10.)

5. If they stumble along the road of recovery, dust off, get up, and keep walking towards their freedom. They may not have immediate perfection, but they must have indomitable persistence.

3 QUALITIES TO CHOOSE IN ORDER TO BE A LEADER

In *Everyone's a Coach*, a book co-authored by the Hall of Fame NFL football coach Don Shula, he writes, "Your game is only as good as your practice."[2] Great teams don't lead their divisions and win championship trophies by chance. Neither do great leaders. To be an extraordinary leader, you must choose to work on developing these 3 uncommon qualities in your life.

1. **The Quality of Repetition.** Many people fail in their goals because it demands doing the same thing right every day, all year long, for the rest of your life. Be persistent in good habits.

2. **The Quality of Creative Thought.** Push your brain. Dare to think an original thought. Great leaders take as

much time to think as they do to act. New thoughts turn into new ideas that turn into new products that turn into new money that turns into new influence.

3. **The Quality of Truth.** Decide right now to always side with truth. Let the eternal Word of God guide all of your choices. A leader never put a wet finger in the air to test the breeze. Great leaders push upwind if necessary.

3 REASONS LEADERSHIP CREATES EVANGELISM

Every person in the world looks for someone else to follow. Someone they can look up to. Someone who's already been where they want to go. If someone like Madonna ever comes to a deep and personal faith in Christ, it will likely be a result of someone in her world that she respects and admires shared the gospel in a relevant way. Who can God use you to influence as a leader in your world? It may be younger classmates at school or people who look up to you because of a certain talent you have developed. Here are some reasons you can evangelize through leadership.

1. **There is a group of people who relate to your interests and respect who you are and what you do.** Out of all the people in the world, you have the best possible opportunity to reach them.

2. **People everywhere admire risk-takers.** That's what a leader does. He or she takes risks by attempting and daring to do things that others stand back and watch.

3. **People have trouble arguing with success.** They may try to argue with your beliefs, but they cannot argue with the success that your beliefs have produced. The success of Jesus' ministry in healing the sick and raising the dead caused people to listen to His message.

3 THINGS THAT WILL MAKE YOU A HUMBLE LEADER

I teased my colleague in ministry awhile back about his abundance of confidence in his own ability. I asked him how his new book was doing. He replied, "Which one are you talking about?" I jabbed back, "The 10 Greatest Men in America and How I Met the Other 9"! While there's nothing wrong with a strong sense of self-worth and personal confidence, it must be tempered with genuine humility. I once heard someone say, "People with humility don't think less of themselves; they just think of themselves less." Here are 3 things to remember about humility.

1. Humble leaders don't diminish their skills and achievements, but they remember to credit their God, their team, and their mentors.

2. Humble leaders make the janitor feel just as important as the vice president in the success of an organization. Every contributing person on a team is critical to its success.

3. Humble leaders are more interested in serving than in being served. Jesus taught us that the greatest in His kingdom must be the servant of all. (Matt. 23:11.)

3 REASONS IT'S COOL TO MAKE GOOD MONEY

In the past, some Christians have believed and taught that all Christians should be poor. Sadly, they have had a very poor understanding of what God says in the Bible. While the Lord is opposed to making money our god and primary focus, He wants to bring finances into our hands for the right purposes. Check out 3 reasons why making good money is cool with Him.

1. **God wants you to learn how to provide well for yourself and your family.** In fact, He says that if you don't make money and provide for your home, you are worse than an infidel (a really bad sinner)! (1 Tim. 5:8.)

2. **God wants you to use your money to sow into His kingdom in order to make provision to take**

the message of Christ around the world. It costs money to print Bibles, support missionaries, and build soul-winning churches. (2 Cor. 9:6-11.)

3. **Simply, God loves His children.** As our Father, He wants to meet all of our needs and even our desires. As long as we keep our eyes and hearts focused on Him, it is His will to bless us abundantly. (Ps. 37:4; Matt. 6:33; Phil. 4:19.)

THE 4 MOST IMPORTANT DESTINATIONS OF EVERY LEADER

Leaders are going somewhere. You can't effectively lead unless you have a vision for a destination that you are headed to. If you fail to keep your eyes on your target, you will fail to lead effectively. Here are 4 critical destination points for every great leader.

1. **Eternal reward.** Every great leader of men should seek to hear the words from our Savior, Jesus Christ, "Well done, good and faithful servant" (Matt. 25:21). Are we doing kingdom work that will please God at the end of our days?

2. **Successors.** You have not truly succeeded as a leader unless you have mentored and raised up a successor. Moses had Joshua. Elijah had Elisha.

Jesus had disciples who carried on His work. Who are you influencing?

3. **Financial overflow.** God wants you to have more than enough money. In fact, that's one of His promises to the tither and giver. (Mal. 3:10.) When you have more than you need, you are in a place to use your extra money for other people and for good works of Christ.

4. **Followers.** I heard a well-known leadership expert say, "If you think you're leading and no one is following, you're just taking a walk." The purpose of leadership is to get as many people as possible on the track you are on. Why? Because you ought to believe you're on the right track. And if you're not sure you're on the right track, you haven't qualified yourself to lead.

ENDNOTES

[1] Maxwell, John. *The 21 Irrefutable Laws of Leadership.* Nashville: Thomas Nelson, 1998.

[2] Ken Blanchard and Don Shula. *Everyone's a Coach.* Grand Rapids: Zondervan, 1996.

PRAYER OF SALVATION

God loves you—no matter who you are, no matter what your past. God loves you so much that He gave His one and only begotten Son for you. The Bible tells us that "…whoever believes in him shall not perish but have eternal life" (John 3:16 NIV). Jesus laid down His life and rose again so that we could spend eternity with Him in heaven and experience His absolute best on earth. If you would like to receive Jesus into your life, say the following prayer out loud and mean it from your heart.

> *Heavenly Father, I come to You admitting that I am a sinner. Right now, I choose to turn away from sin, and I ask You to cleanse me of all unrighteousness. I believe that Your Son, Jesus, died on the cross to take away my sins. I also believe that He rose again from the dead so that I might be forgiven of my sins and made righteous through faith in Him. I call upon the name of Jesus Christ to be the Savior and Lord of my life. Jesus, I choose to follow You and ask that You fill me with the power of the Holy Spirit. I declare that right now I am a child of God. I am free from sin and full of the righteousness of God. I am saved in Jesus' name. Amen.*

If you prayed this prayer to receive Jesus Christ as your Savior for the first time, please contact us on the web at **www.harrisonhouse.com** to receive a free book.

Or you may write to us at
Harrison House
P.O. Box 35035
Tulsa, Oklahoma 74153

ABOUT THE AUTHOR

Blaine Bartel founded Thrive Communications, an organization dedicated to serving those who shape the local church. He is also currently leading a new church launch in a growing area of north Dallas.

Bartel was the founding youth pastor and one of the key strategists in the creation of Oneighty, which has become one of the most emulated youth ministries in the past decade reaching 2,500 – 3,000 students weekly under his leadership. In a tribute to the long term effects and influence of Blaine's leadership, hundreds of young people that grew up under his ministry are now serving in full time ministry themselves.

A recognized authority on the topics of youth ministry and successful parenting, Bartel is a best-selling author with 12 books published in 4 languages, and is the creator of Thrive—one of the most listened to youth ministry development systems in the country, selling more than 100,000 audio tapes and cd's worldwide. He is one of the most sought after speakers in his field; more than one million people from over 40 countries have attended Blaine Bartel's live seminars or speaking engagements.

His work has been featured in major media including "The Washington Post," CBS' "The Early Show," "The 700 Club," "Seventeen" magazine, as well as newspapers, radio programs, and Internet media worldwide.

Bartel's commitment to creating an enduring legacy that will impact the world is surpassed only by his passion for family as a dedicated father of three children and a loving husband to his wife of more than 20 years, Cathy.

To contact Blaine Bartel,

write:

Blaine Bartel

Serving America's Future

P.O. Box 691923

Tulsa, OK 74169

www.blainebartel.com

Please include your prayer requests

and comments when you write.

To contact Oneighty®, write:

Oneighty®

P.O. Box 770

Tulsa, OK 74101

www.Oneighty.com

OTHER BOOKS BY BLAINE BARTEL

every teenager's
Little Black Book
on reaching your dreams

every teenager's
Little Black Book
on how to get along with your parents

every teenager's
Little Black Book
of God's guarantees

every teenager's
Little Black Book
for athletes

every teenager's
Little Black Book
on cash

every teenager's
Little Black Book
on cool

every teenager's
Little Black Book
on sex and dating

every teenager's
Little Black Book
of hard to find information

Little Black Book
for graduates

Thrive Teen Devotional

The Big Black Book
for parents

**Let Me Tell You What
Your Teens Are Telling Me**

7 Absolutes to Pray Over Your Kids

For more information on the *little black book* series
please visit our website at: **www.littleblackbooks.info**

Available at fine bookstores everywhere
or at **www.harrisonhouse.com**

Take the Turn for God in Just 5 Minutes a Day

Witty, short, and inspiring devotions for teens from one of America's youth leadership specialists!

Teens can discover a real, action-packed, enthusiastic relationship with God. The thrive.teen.devotional is motivated by a very simple challenge: Give just five minutes a day to God and watch your life turn around.

At the end of eight weeks, the Word of God is going to be more real and alive to teens than ever before as they gain spiritual insights on issues like friendships, self-esteem, and prayer. The good news is that when one's mind is renewed, they experience a radical turnaround in every other area of their life, too.

thrive.teen.devotional
by Blaine Bartel
1-57794-777-0

Available at bookstores everywhere or visit www.harrisonhouse.com

daughters are sugar and spice and everything nice...

well, most of the time!

being mommy or daddy's little *princess* can get challenging sometimes. plug into God's Word and discover what it means to be your heavenly Father's daughter and how special you are to your "fam."

stories, humor, scriptures...everything you need to become the lovely and hip *lady* God has destined you to be.

Available at fine bookstores everywhere or at **www.harrisonhouse.com**.

Harrison House
ISBN: 1-57794-792-4

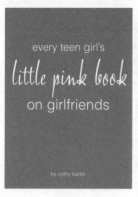

every teen girl's
little pink book
on girlfriends

by cathy bartel

find out how you can be a friend to the end...

girlfriends are great!

- wild and crazy,
- quiet and thoughtful,
- fun and exciting.

you can start being a true "girlfriend" to your gal pals:

learn the ropes

get the inside scoop

navigate clichés

stick together

learn to be real

Available at fine bookstores everywhere or at **www.harrisonhouse.com**.

Harrison House
ISBN: 1-57794-794-0

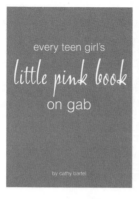

girls about to become

what you think about, you **gab** about, you bring about. you will become what you say.

launch your destiny simply by the things you say. discover how to lay a foundation of success for your future through your words – in love, in school, in relationships, in life. become something great!

Available at fine bookstores everywhere or at **www.harrisonhouse.com**.

Harrison House
ISBN: 1-57794-793-2

God ideas for a great wardrobe

every teen girl's little pink book on what to wear

by cathy bartel

find out what's hot:

- cool clothes
- faith
- smiles
- beauty inside
- modesty
- God's love

fashion sense. personal style. get them both.

Available at fine bookstores everywhere or at **www.harrisonhouse.com**.

Harrison House
ISBN: 1-57794-795-9

Fast. Easy. Convenient.

For the latest Harrison House product information and author news, look no further than your computer. All the details on our powerful, life-changing products are just a click away. New releases, E-mail subscriptions, Podcasts, testimonies, monthly specials—find it all in one place. Visit harrisonhouse.com today!

harrisonhouse

THE HARRISON HOUSE VISION

Proclaiming the truth and the power

Of the Gospel of Jesus Christ

With excellence;

Challenging Christians to

Live victoriously,

Grow spiritually,

Know God intimately.